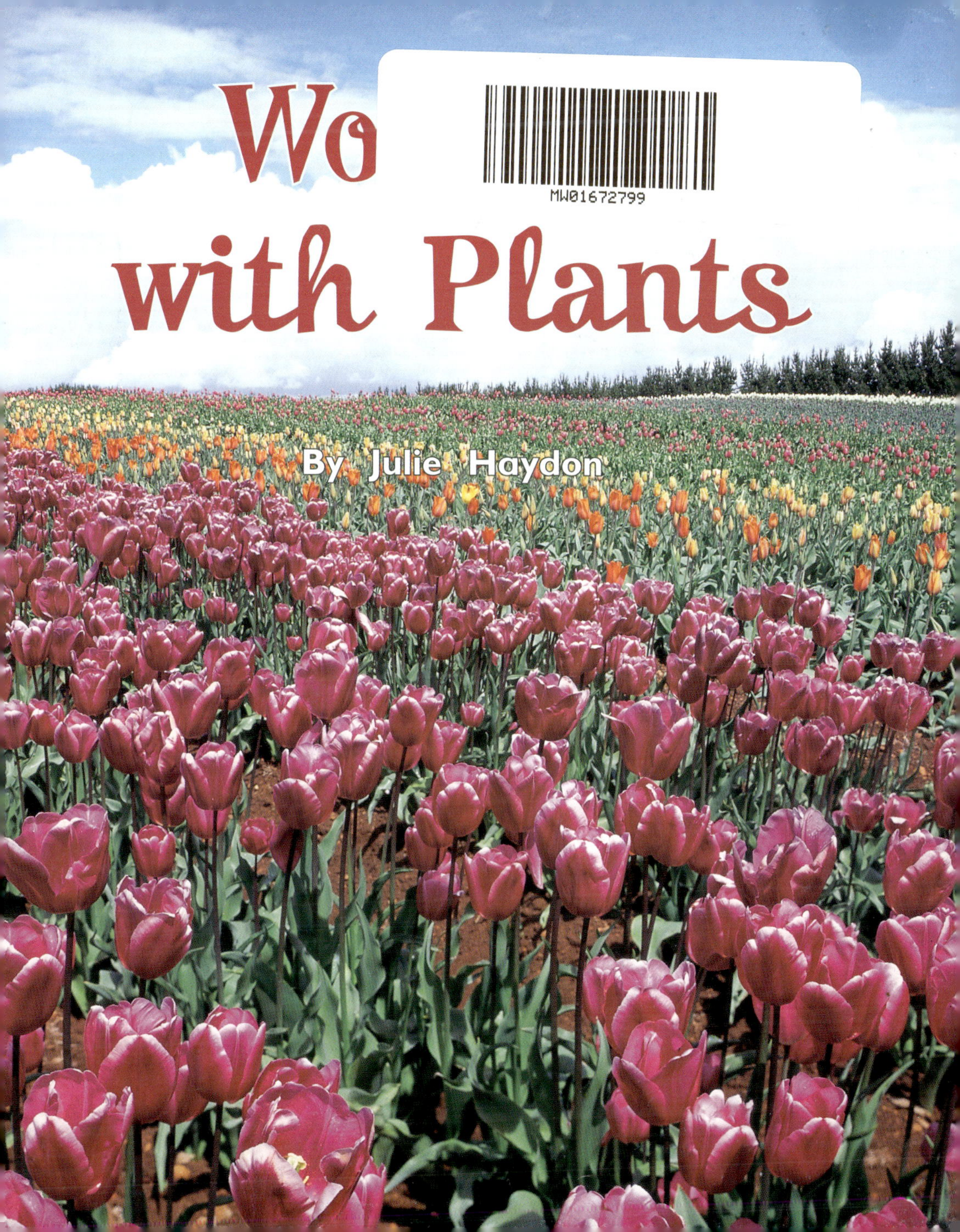

Wo
with Plants

By Julie Haydon

Plants

We need plants.
We eat plants.
We make things
from plants.
Plants help to keep
the air clean.

Working with Plants

Lots of people work with plants.

Some people grow plants.

Some people sell plants.

Some people take care of plants.

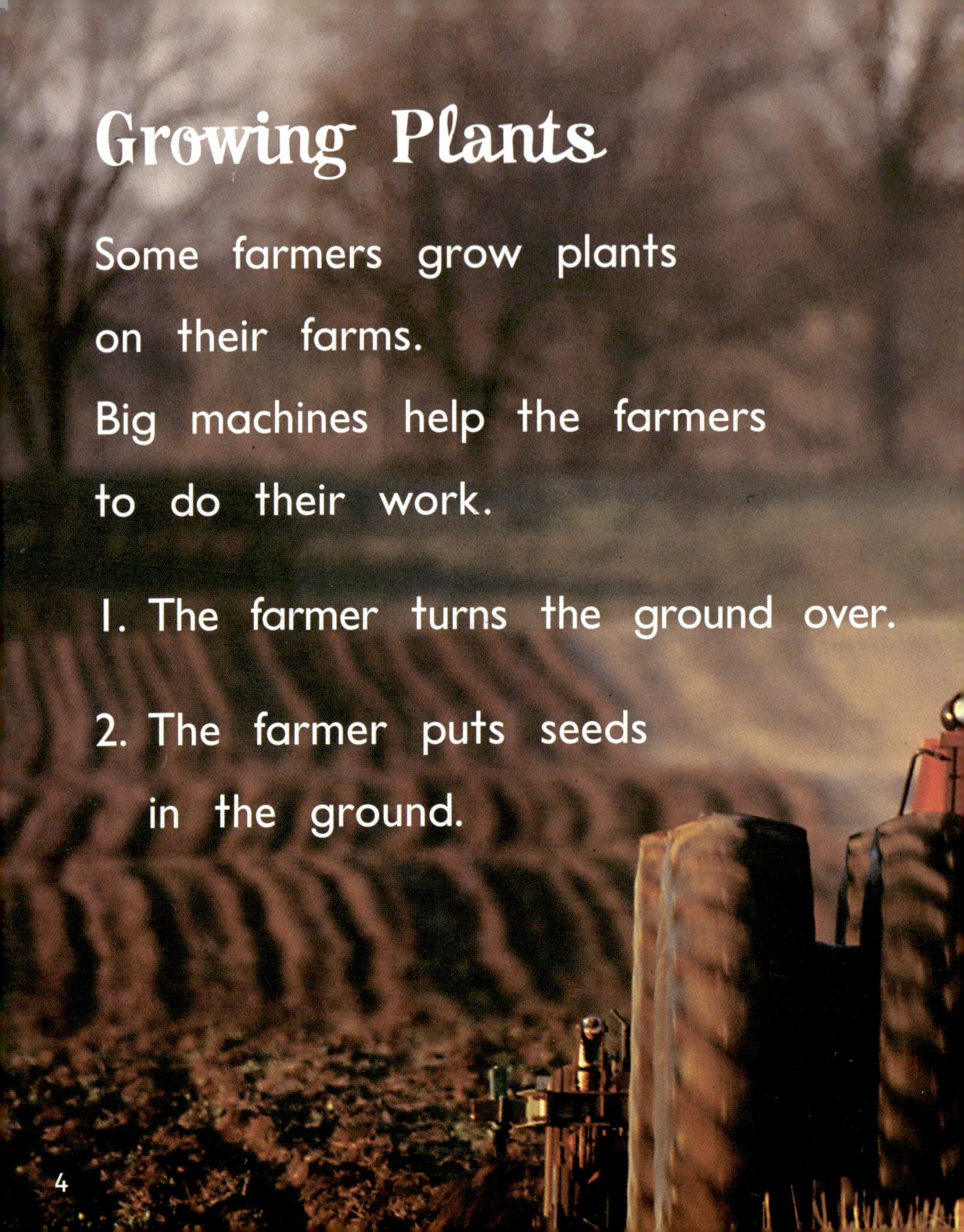

Growing Plants

Some farmers grow plants
on their farms.
Big machines help the farmers
to do their work.

1. The farmer turns the ground over.
2. The farmer puts seeds
   in the ground.

3. The farmer looks after the plants.

4. The farmer cuts
or picks the plants.

The Wheat Farmer

Some farmers grow wheat.

The wheat goes to a factory and is made into flour.

Bread, pasta, and other foods are made with flour.

The Cotton Farmer

Some farmers grow cotton.

The cotton goes to a factory
to be cleaned.

The cotton is made into cloth.

Jeans and shirts
are made from cloth.

The Vegetable Farmer

Some farmers grow vegetables.

Some vegetables go to a store.
Some vegetables go to a factory
and are put into cans and bags.

Growing other Plants

Here are some other plants that people grow.

Selling Plants

Some people sell plants.

1. The plants come
   to the store.

2. The plants
   are put in the store
   so that people
   can see them.

3. People buy
   the plants.

The Florist

A florist sells plants
and flowers in a store.

People buy the plants and flowers
to put in their homes.
Some people give plants
and flowers as presents.

The Grocer

A grocer sells fruit
and vegetables in a store.

People buy the fruit
and vegetables to eat.

B

Taking Care of Plants

Some people take care of plants.

1. They keep plants healthy.
2. They grow new plants.
3. They keep parks, gardens, and forests looking good.

The Gardener

A gardener takes care
of the plants
in a garden or park.

People like to visit
gardens and parks.
Some people have gardens at home.

The Forester

A forester takes care of the plants and animals in a forest.

The trees give us wood.
We make things from wood.

People like to visit forests, too.